KIDNAPPING AND PIRACY

by Judith Anderson

A+

Smart Apple Media

Published by Smart Apple Media
P.O. Box 3263, Mankato, Minnesota 56002

Printed in the United States of America at
Corporate Graphics, in North Mankato, Minnesota.

Published by arrangement with the
Watts Publishing Group LTD, London.

Library of Congress Cataloging-in-Publication Data

Anderson, Judith
Kidnapping and piracy / Judith Anderson.
p. cm.—(Inside crime)
Includes index.
Summary: "Delves into the criminal world of
modern-day shipping piracy, along with hostage
taking. Also describes motives of kidnapping
in general. Explains tactics of law enforcement
agencies to recover victims and prevent the
crime"—Provided by publisher.
ISBN 978-1-59920-398-0 (library binding)
1. Pirates—Juvenile literature. 2. Piracy—
Case studies—Juvenile literature. 3. Political
kidnapping—Juvenile literature. 4. Hijacking
of ships—Prevention—Juvenile literature.
5. Kidnapping—Juvenile literature. I. Title.
G535.H79 2012
364.16'4—dc22
                                    2011004296

Series editor: Jeremy Smith
Editor: Julia Bird
Design: sprout.uk.com
Artworks: sprout.uk.com
Picture researcher: Diana Morris

Picture credits: AFP/Getty Images: 30. Hassan
Ammar/AP/PAI: 17t. AP/PAI: 11, 29.
AP/Topfoto: 28.Rodrigo Arangua/AFP/Getty Images:
27. Eric L Beauregard/Landor/PAI: 19.
Bridgeman Art Library/Getty Images: 10. Ben
Churchill/AFP/Getty Images: 40. Frederic Courbet/
Panos: 15. Mohamed Dahar/AFP/Getty Images: 13t.
Jay Directo/AFP/Getty Images: 35t. EPA/Corbis: 23.
Christopher Furlong/Getty Images: 25.
Kansas Association of Hostage Negotiators: 34.
Tony Karumba/AFP/Getty Images: 20.
KPA/ZUMA/Rex Features: front cover cr.
Louis Lanzio/AP/PAI: 21. Paul Madej/AP/PAI: 18.
David McNew/Getty Images: 33. Stephen Morton/
Getty Images: 39. Dieter Nagl/Getty Images: 41.
NTV/AFP/Getty Images: 36. nullplus/istockphoto: 8.
Spencer Platt/Getty Images: 32. Photo Courtesy
Plymouth County Jail/Getty Images: 31. Mark
Ralston/AFP/Getty Images: 24. Rex Features: 26,
35b. Paul J Richards/Getty Images: 38. Yuli Seperi/
AFP/Getty Images: 13b. David Silverman/Getty
Images: 9b. Sipa Press/Rex Features: front cover b,
5, 9t, 37. Arthur Turner/Alamy: front cover cl.
U.S. Navy photo by Air Crewman 2nd Class David
B.Hudson/released: 16, 17b. Farh Abdi Warsameh/
AP/PAI: 14.

1306
3-2011

9 8 7 6 5 4 3 2 1

CONTENTS

Piracy and kidnapping are two of the world's oldest forms of crime. Piracy involves theft and violence at sea, while kidnapping is the illegal capture and detention of people against their will. These two crimes are quite distinct, yet they can overlap; pirates frequently kidnap passengers and crew, as well as seize vessels and goods.

Piracy

Piracy is all about profit. Pirates prey on vessels at sea, using force to make an illegal boarding. They may seize goods from commercial ships, the private possessions of crew and passengers, or the vessel itself. Policing pirates is an immensely difficult task because of the vastness of the world's oceans and waterways. Also, few countries have adequate laws to deal with pirates, and many incidents occur in international waters beyond the jurisdiction of individual states.

▼ *Ships like this big oil tanker can become easy targets for pirates when far out at sea.*

FACT FILE

Some estimates suggest that as few as one in ten incidents of kidnapping or piracy are officially reported. This may be because family members are afraid of what kidnappers will do to their loved ones if the police are alerted. The companies whose workers or vessels or cargo are seized know that their insurance costs will rise dramatically if they inform the authorities. It may seem easier to accept the loss or pay any ransom (see page 9) privately.

BUSTED!

A millionaire businessman and his family were rescued by police in Shanghai, China in 2009 after a man demanding a ransom held them at gunpoint in their own home. Police negotiated with the hostage taker, while secretly gaining access to the house. Meanwhile, a second rescue team rehearsed the rescue in a nearby house with the same layout, so they could spot any problems in advance. After 24 hours, the first team shot the hostage taker dead. The family was freed unharmed.

▲ Police rescue operations can be very risky. This picture shows the aftermath of a battle to free over 1,100 people held hostage at a school in Beslan, North Ossetia in 2004. More than 300 hostages were killed and many more were injured.

▶ BBC journalist Alan Johnson was kidnapped in the Gaza Strip in 2007 by a Muslim extremist group demanding the release of Muslim prisoners in the UK. He was released unharmed 16 weeks later.

Kidnapping

Profit is also one of the most common motives for kidnapping. The kidnappers demand money, known as a ransom, in exchange for the safe return of the victim. However, kidnapping is a complex crime and its perpetrators may have other motives, such as revenge for family grievances, sexual abuse or enslavement, political or military aims, or simply to publicize extremist views.

Policing the crime of kidnapping is particularly sensitive, because an armed response from law enforcement agencies may endanger the lives of the victims. Police forces and governments are usually very reluctant to give in to the kidnappers' demands, as this sends a signal that kidnappers can hold people to ransom and get away with it.

IN THE PAST

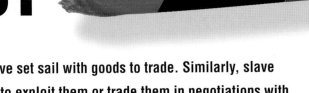

Thieves have attacked vessels for as long as men have set sail with goods to trade. Similarly, slave traders, bandits, and warriors have captured people to exploit them or trade them in negotiations with their enemies for thousands of years. In 75 BC, the great Roman emperor Julius Caesar was kidnapped by pirates in the eastern Mediterranean. He was freed unharmed after a ransom was paid.

Pirate Economies

Today, piracy is a crime in international law and no country openly promotes it. But in the past, towns, islands, or even whole states built their economy through raiding parties at sea. Viking raiders from Scandinavia plundered coasts freely throughout western and northern Europe from the 8th to the 11th centuries. Some states even allowed pirates, known as privateers, to capture their enemies' ships and share the treasure. A famous 16th century English privateer, Sir Francis Drake, sailed around the world, raiding many Spanish vessels along the way. He gave Queen Elizabeth I of England half of his captured cargo.

Slavery and Press-Gangs

The transatlantic slave trade grew from the trading of victims kidnapped along the West African coast and sold into a life of slavery working on plantations in the newly colonized Americas. This cruel and barbaric practice was officially sanctioned by both the United Kingdom and the United States until the early 19th century. Many navies and commercial fleets also enslaved people from their own countries and elsewhere by kidnapping or "press-ganging" them onto ships where they were forced to work for very little or no pay.

▼ *This 17th century painting shows Barbary pirates from North Africa attacking a Spanish ship.*

Hostages in War

Kidnapping or hostage-taking is a routine weapon of war. High profile prisoners can bring a significant ransom, or be used to secure the release of prisoners held by the enemy. In the 20th century, hostage-taking was common in conflicts from the Spanish Civil War to the first Iraq War. Civilian hostages provided human shields as protection against attack, or were killed to serve as a warning to the enemy. However, taking civilian hostages in wartime is now considered to be an illegal act under international law. This is because civilian communities should not be punished or held responsible for military actions.

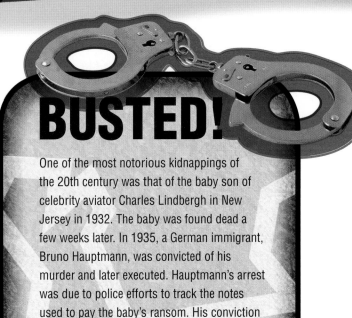

BUSTED!

One of the most notorious kidnappings of the 20th century was that of the baby son of celebrity aviator Charles Lindbergh in New Jersey in 1932. The baby was found dead a few weeks later. In 1935, a German immigrant, Bruno Hauptmann, was convicted of his murder and later executed. Hauptmann's arrest was due to police efforts to track the notes used to pay the baby's ransom. His conviction rested on circumstantial evidence, such as the similarity between handwriting on the ransom letters and Hauptmann's own handwriting.

▼ Bruno Hauptmann (center), convicted of the kidnapping and murder of baby Charles Lindbergh, Jr., enters prison to await his execution in 1935.

PIRACY AT SEA

Over 90 percent of world trade cargo is carried by ships at sea. Much of it is transported via container ships or supertankers—huge vessels as big as aircraft carriers. The routes used by these vessels pass through vast areas of open ocean that do not lie within the jurisdiction of any one country, yet most incidents of modern piracy occur in just a few locations.

Where in the World?

Pirates need a coast from which to launch their boats, and a supply of ships to attack. Most pirate activity occurs in areas of heavy commercial shipping with easy access to a coastline that is poorly policed due to poverty, corruption, or civil war. Such areas include the east coast of Africa, West Africa's Gulf of Guinea, the South China Sea, and areas of the Pacific.

▼ *This map of international shipping lanes shows how most commercial maritime vessels use the same routes. This makes it easy for pirates to predict where those vessels will be.*

Motives

Local groups of pirates may attack fishing boats, yachts, or smaller cargo ships simply to steal property from their safes or crews. Similarly, they may aim to kidnap the crew or passengers in the hope of a ransom. They are looking for a quick profit. However, piracy in the Gulf of Aden off the east coast of Africa is increasingly attracting the attention of organized criminal gangs who may use the extensive ransom payouts from targeting large commercial vessels to pay off officials, fund lavish lifestyles, or promote civil war or acts of terrorism.

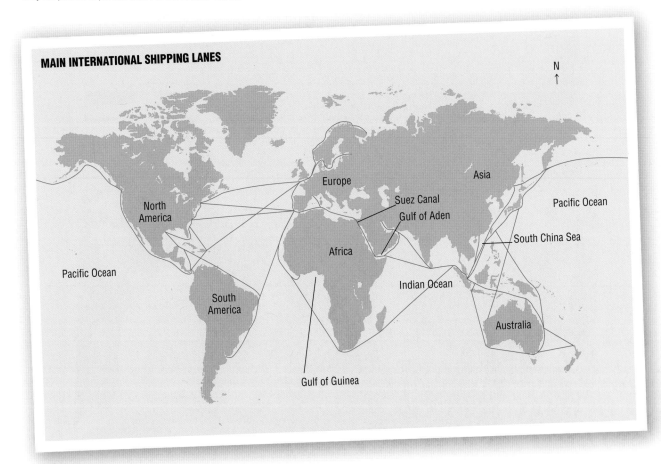

MAIN INTERNATIONAL SHIPPING LANES

N ↑

Europe

Asia

Suez Canal

Gulf of Aden

Pacific Ocean

North America

South China Sea

Africa

Pacific Ocean

Indian Ocean

South America

Australia

Gulf of Guinea

▲ *Armed pirates prepare to launch their boat from the Somali coast. From here, the busy Gulf of Aden is close by.*

Pirate Tactics

In order to attack a vessel, pirates must have boats of their own. Local pirate groups may use small fishing vessels to disguise their weapons. They might claim their boat has broken down and call for assistance from passing ships. This enables them to approach larger vessels. More organized and better-funded groups of pirates may operate from a "mother ship," using advanced tracking technology to find targets and send out small speedboats armed with sophisticated rocket launchers to surround the vessel and force it to submit.

The Crew

A successful attack can depend on the careful selection of pirate crew: ex-soldiers for "muscle" and weaponry, fishermen with good knowledge of local waters, and someone who can use GPS technology.

ON TARGET

A narrow channel of water known as the Malacca Strait in southeast Asia used to be the world's most pirate-prone region in the world until 2004, when Indonesia, Malaysia, and Singapore began to coordinate their responses to the problem. After several months of joint naval air and sea patrols, the pirate attacks on commercial shipping were reduced by about sixty percent.

▶ *An Indonesian soldier stands guard near a U.S. Navy flagship during a 2006 visit in Indonesia to share information on shipping safety in the Malacca Strait.*

SOMALIA

The Gulf of Aden off the coast of Somalia is of huge strategic importance for international shipping. Nearly 20,000 ships pass through the area each year, heading for the Suez Canal that connects Europe and Asia. Many of these ships carry vital oil supplies from the Middle East to destinations all around the world. Others carry essential food aid and supplies to poverty-stricken regions of East Africa. In 2009, over half of all pirate attacks worldwide took place here.

An Unstable State

Somalia has been fighting a civil war since 1991. The region, already poor and undeveloped, has suffered huge setbacks in security and a stable government. Many different rebel factions control large areas of the coast, so pirate groups have been able to emerge and expand without interference from the police, the navy, or the coastguard.

▼ Somali rebel fighters on the streets of the capital Mogadishu, Somalia in 2010. A long-running civil war in the country has left Somalians divided and poverty-stricken.

Controversy over Causes

Several reports published by the United Nations have pointed to a history of illegal fishing and the dumping of toxic waste by other nations in the seas around Somalia. This is believed to have seriously affected the livelihoods of Somali fishermen, who in the face of these difficulties, have turned to piracy. Others argue that the factions fighting in the war have promoted piracy to fund their activities and maintain their control over the coastline.

▲ *Fishermen pull in their boat near the coastal town of Eyl in Somalia. The town is a base for pirates, and piracy now fuels the local economy as polluted waters off Somalia have made the traditional livelihood of fishing too dangerous.*

Pirate Boom Towns

Such activity has created pirate boom towns around the northeast coast of Africa, with investors providing the cash for raids while gangs spend ransom money, trade stolen cargoes, and deal in the weapons used to attack ships. There is little incentive here for the reintroduction of law and order. Hijacked ships are regularly anchored at ports such as Eyl where pirates simply contact the ship's owners and demand a ransom without fear of capture. The average ransom paid by foreign owners is around $2 million in cash. This is still only a small fraction of the value of the ships themselves or their huge cargoes of oil.

FACT FILE

Recorded acts of piracy and armed robbery off the coast of East Africa:

2006:   31
2007:   60
2008: 134
2009: 222

CASE STUDY: MV *SIRIUS STAR*

In November 2008, the Saudi-owned supertanker MV *Sirius Star* was captured by Somali pirates in the Indian Ocean on its way to the United States. The supertanker was carrying two million barrels of crude oil with a value of $100 million. The crew of 25 was kidnapped along with the hijacked vessel.

Careful Planning

The capture of the *Sirius Star* was a carefully planned operation, which began several days before the main attack with the pirates capturing a Nigerian tug boat to use as a mother ship. The tug provided suitable disguise for the pirates' speedboats and enabled them to travel far out into the Indian Ocean, away from international patrols. Once the location of the *Sirius Star* was established, two speedboats and up to 12 pirates with rocket-propelled grenades and machine guns closed in on the vessel. The pirates used ropes to climb aboard the tanker, which was low in the water due to its full load.

FACT FILE

The *Sirius Star* weighs 350,500 tons (318,000 t)—three times the size of an aircraft carrier. It is the largest ship ever to be captured by pirates.

It was captured 518 miles (833 km) from land, farther from the Somali coast than any previous attack.

None of the pirates involved in this attack have been caught.

▶ MV Sirius Star *can carry enough oil to supply the needs of a country the size of France for a day.*

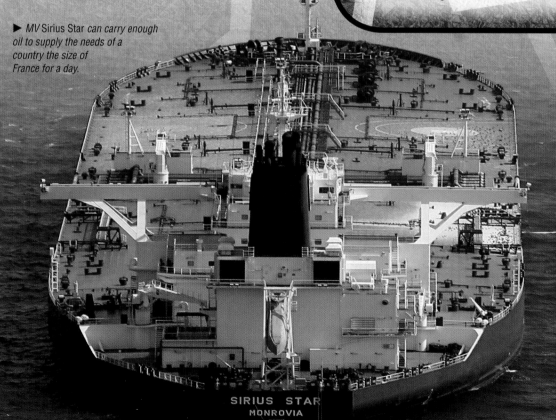

Negotiating the Ransom

The captured ship was forced to head for the Somali coast and was anchored near the port of Harardhere, known to be a pirate stronghold. The pirates then contacted the ship's owners to demand a ransom payment of $25 million. An intense period of negotiation followed. The captured crew included two British men, but the British government insisted that it would not be involved in any ransom payment because it believed this merely encouraged further hostage-taking.

Eventually, the pirates reduced their demands to $3 million, and the ransom was paid by the ship's Saudi owners. The pirates released the crew unharmed and escaped from the ship in a number of small boats. Five of the pirates were reported to have drowned in a storm before they reached the shore.

▲ *Hussein al-Hamza (right), a 24-year-old sailor from the hijacked MV* Sirius Star, *is greeted by a well-wisher as he arrives home in Saudi Arabia.*

▼ *The ransom payment is parachuted onto the deck of the MV* Sirius Star.

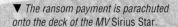

A Shift in Direction

The attack on the MV *Sirius Star* signaled a change in tactics by Somali pirates. Pirates now had greater resources to mount attacks, and their range was extending much farther in order to avoid the international anti-piracy forces already patrolling the Gulf of Aden. Clearly, the international community needed to respond in new ways if it wanted to protect its shipping in the area. Several task forces have recently been established with a range of powers and jurisdictions specifically to tackle this growing problem (see pages 18–19).

POLICING THE PIRATES

Individual countries are usually responsible for policing their own coastal waters. However, poorer countries such as Somalia don't always have an adequate coastguard or navy to carry out the necessary patrols. Also, acts of piracy often occur in international waters. So, an international response is required to deter acts of piracy, and to catch and prosecute the criminals when a ship is hijacked.

Coastal Waters

In 2008, the United Nations Security Council passed a resolution allowing non-Somali naval vessels to enforce the international laws of the sea in Somali territorial waters. This means that, in theory at least, the waters along the coast can no longer be considered a "safe haven" for local pirates.

International Patrols

Many countries with shipping interests in the Gulf of Aden have sent naval vessels to the region in an effort to deter pirate activity. These include China, Russia, and India. In 2008, the European Union's joint naval force in the area launched Operation Atalanta which is specifically tasked to protect vulnerable shipping and escort World Food Programme aid shipments to East Africa.

ON TARGET

The International Maritime Organization reports that while attacks on vessels continue, successful hijackings have been reduced from one in three to one in ten between 2008 and 2010. This is due to a combination of successful evasion tactics by commercial shipping and increased naval patrols in the area.

◄ Combat ready soldiers on a speedboat during an exercise for Swedish ships participating in Operation Atalanta in Somalia.

▲ Members of a "visit, board, search, and seizure" team working for Combined Task Force 151 capture a ship of suspected pirates.

Combined Task Force 151

In 2009, an international naval task force known as Combined Task Force 151 was set up to take a much more proactive role in deterring pirates. Under a central command that rotates between different countries, Task Force ships monitor boats across more than 617,000 sq miles (1.6 million sq km) of the Indian Ocean and check for suspicious items, such as ladders, grappling hooks, and weapons that have no place on ordinary fishing vessels. They have also established a narrow transit corridor in the Gulf of Aden. This corridor is more heavily patrolled than elsewhere, giving ships who use it a greater degree of protection.

BUSTED!

In April 2010, the flagship of Combined Task Force 151, USS *Farragut*, intercepted suspected pirates after they were alerted to an attack on the oil tanker MV *Evita* off the coast of Somalia. The MV *Evita* managed to escape by increasing its speed and firing flares at the pirates, whose skiffs were located and monitored by a helicopter from the USS *Farragut*. The skiffs were boarded and searched, their grappling hooks were removed, and the mother skiff was sunk. The pirates were then released. No further action was taken because of a lack of the necessary evidence to secure a conviction (see page 20).

PROSECUTION AND DETENTION

Despite recent successes in thwarting pirate attacks, relatively few pirates end up in court. This is partly because of the difficulty in gathering evidence—a grappling hook on a skiff may suggest intent to board a ship illegally, but this cannot be proved. However, even when pirates are caught red-handed, there's no point in arresting them if the necessary police, prisons, and justice systems aren't in place on shore.

Shipriders

Ideally, suspects should be tried in their own country or in the country that owns the hijacked ship. But in the case of Somalian pirates, the Somali justice system has been weakened by the war and many of the ship-owning countries are too far away. These pirates cannot easily be tried in Europe because European law insists there should be no more than a few hours' delay between the arrest of a suspect and the start of legal proceedings. So the UN has promoted the use of "shipriders"—law enforcement officers from neighboring countries such as Kenya who join foreign patrolling ships and are on hand to facilitate swift and effective arrests and evidence gathering.

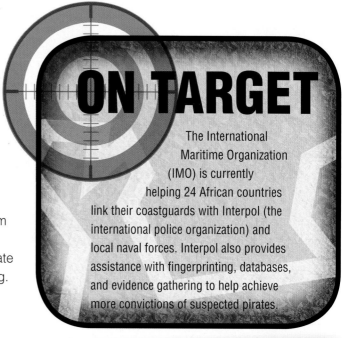

ON TARGET

The International Maritime Organization (IMO) is currently helping 24 African countries link their coastguards with Interpol (the international police organization) and local naval forces. Interpol also provides assistance with fingerprinting, databases, and evidence gathering to help achieve more convictions of suspected pirates.

▼ *Suspected Somali pirates wait for their trial to begin at a specially built courthouse on the grounds of Shimo la Tewa Prison in Mombasa, Kenya in 2010.*

Regional Courts

Kenya, just to the south of Somalia, originally agreed to hold and prosecute pirates arrested in the region. However, the burden has proved too much for Kenya's already overloaded judicial system so, in 2010, the island country of Seychelles agreed to amend its laws and allow its courts to prosecute pirates from other countries. But this will not solve the problem in the long term. The Seychelles has only two courtrooms and very little prison capacity.

Other Solutions?

Most people accept that the only viable long term solution is to assist the Somali government in creating a stronger police and judicial system so that it can deal with its own criminals. However, this won't happen overnight, and in the meantime some Western states are looking at ways to bring their own

▼ Convicted pirate 18-year-old Abdiwali Abdiqadir Muse (see Busted box) is led into court in New York in 2009.

prosecutions against pirates who attack their ships. In May 2010, the trial of five Somali men accused of attempting to hijack a Dutch-registered ship began in the Netherlands. It was the first piracy trial in Europe to result from the recent wave of attacks in the Gulf of Aden.

BUSTED!

The United States recently tried a Somali man charged with hijacking the U.S. ship *Maersk Alabama* off Somalia in April 2009 and kidnapping its captain. Abdiwali Abdiqadir Muse was the only pirate to survive the attack after snipers killed his companions. He faces a minimum of 27 years in prison.

KIDNAPPING FOR RANSOM

Estimates suggest that more than 30,000 kidnappings take place worldwide each year. The numbers are uncertain because many kidnappings go unreported. But whatever the figures, kidnapping is a serious crime that can devastate families, and in some parts of the world, cause whole communities to live in fear.

The Victims

Kidnapping for ransom is about making money. Very rich people may feel themselves to be targets because they are known to have the means to pay out a big ransom. But often victims are chosen because they are "soft" targets with less wealth, and also with less security than more high profile figures. These people may include employees, such as engineers who work for foreign mining companies, local businesspeople, and ordinary people with some savings. Around 90 percent of all kidnapping victims are locals, not foreigners.

BUSTED!

A group of kidnappers was arrested in Chihuahua, Mexico, in 2010 after kidnapping two young women and abusing them to convince their families that a ransom had to be paid. The group, known as Los Rojas, was caught when police organized the delivery of a fake ransom payment. The two victims were successfully rescued.

▼ Kidnapping hotspots around the world include Afghanistan, Colombia, Iraq, Mexico, Nigeria, Pakistan, the Philippines, and Somalia. All of these countries suffer from weak law enforcement, social deprivation, and widespread corruption.

KIDNAPPING HOTSPOTS

N
↑

Afghanistan
Iraq
Pakistan
Mexico
Nigeria
the Philippines
Colombia
Somalia

Proof of Life

Once a victim is kidnapped, their abductors seek to negotiate a ransom with family members or the company who employs them. They will often send a "proof of life"—a video or a tape recording, for example, to show that their victims are still alive. Negotiations may last for a few hours, weeks, or even months.

Express Kidnapping

Sometimes kidnappers don't even bother to demand a ransom from a third party. They simply drive their victim to a cash machine and force them to withdraw money. The profits may be smaller, but the kidnapping is over very quickly and the overhead is much less. This is known as "express kidnapping." It is particularly common in urban areas of Mexico, Colombia, Venezuela, and Brazil.

▼ *Members of Mexico's anti-kidnapping police squad raid a property in search of suspected kidnappers in Nezahualcoyotl in 2010.*

An Under-reported Crime

In many instances of kidnapping, family members don't inform the police or the media out of fear of a bungled rescue attempt or punishment for the victim. Some security firms estimate that up to 70 percent of all kidnappings are resolved by private payment of a ransom, while only 10 percent of victims are rescued. In countries where corruption is prevalent, the police may actually take bribes to turn a blind eye to the crime.

ON TARGET

After the brutal kidnapping and murder of a 14-year-old boy in Mexico in 2008, the Mexican authorities launched an anti-kidnapping police squad consisting of around 300 officers who receive special training. The officers take regular honesty pledges in an effort to avoid accusations of corruption.

ABDUCTING CHILDREN

Children are abducted, or kidnapped, for all sorts of reasons. Often it is for ransom, as the horror of a kidnapped child makes families more likely to pay up. Sometimes children are abducted in a battle over custody rights or in cases of child abuse. But sometimes a child is preferred over an adult simply because they are easier to take and hide.

Victims of Abuse

No one knows for sure how many children are abducted and imprisoned in the developing countries of the world, but kidnappings in developed countries tend to generate a lot of media attention. These abductions are less likely to be for financial gain and are often associated with abusers or pedophiles who may have no intention of ever handing the victim back to his or her family.

◀ *Eleven-year-old Jaycee Dugard was abducted from a bus stop in her home town of South Lake Tahoe, California, in 1991 by Phillip and Nancy Garrido. They kept her hidden in their backyard for 18 years before she was finally discovered by police.*

ON TARGET

The Amber Alert program was established in the United States after the abduction and murder of nine-year-old Amber Hagerman in 1996. This voluntary partnership between law-enforcement agencies, broadcasters, and transportation agencies is designed to activate an urgent bulletin in the most serious child-abduction cases, passing on a description of the child and any information about their abductor to the entire community as quickly as possible.

Child Trafficking

Many thousands of children are abducted every year and transported to another region or another country in order to work for no pay in sweat shops or brothels. Thousands of others are sold for adoption to wealthy families. The motive behind their abduction is pure profit, and few of the children will ever see their families again. Most of these children are from developing countries or have been displaced by war or famine. However, the criminals who exploit them come from every country in the world, including the United States and countries in Europe.

Custody Battles

When parents divorce, they usually reach an agreement about where their children will live. But sometimes parents can't agree. One parent may abduct their own children and take them to another country where the child custody laws are different and the rights of the other parent are not recognized. This type of abduction is known as international parental child abduction (IPCA). The U.S. State Department's Office of Child Issues received 1,135 requests for assistance in IPCA cases involving U.S. children in 2009, though it is estimated that many thousands more cases go unreported.

BUSTED!

Five-year-old British boy Sahil Saeed was kidnapped while on vacation in Pakistan in March 2010. A huge ransom was demanded, but his captors were caught when they instructed the boy's uncle to return to the UK to raise the money. This enabled Pakistani officials and the British Serious Organised Crime Agency (SOCA) to work together to set a trap for the kidnappers in a surveillance operation that also involved French and Spanish police. Two weeks later, Sahil was found safe and well, and returned to his family.

▶ Sahil Saeed is reunited with his mother in March 2010 following his kidnap ordeal.

TAKEN HOSTAGE

Kidnapping may have become a lucrative industry in some parts of the world, but not every kidnapper is seeking a ransom. Some are motivated by religion, ideology, fear, or hatred. Their victims are usually referred to as hostages, and their capture and detention is often called a hostage crisis.

Human Shields

Sometimes hostages are seized as "human shields" to deter the police or military from armed response or attack. Certainly, a hostage crisis alters the response of the police or military in any incident or conflict. They must proceed with extreme caution in order to minimize the risk to innocent people. After his invasion of Kuwait in 1990, former Iraqi President Saddam Hussein detained hundreds of foreign civilians, including children, and paraded them on TV to deter a military attack by western nations, including the United States.

Militant Groups

Groups of guerrilla fighters or militants sometimes seize hostages in order to publicize their cause and demand concessions, such as the release of political prisoners. They may target high profile individuals such as politicians or simply seize people opportunistically. Hostages held in these circumstances often face a particularly lengthy ordeal, as few governments are prepared to openly give in to their enemy's demands.

▼ *Iraqi leader Saddam Hussein appears on TV with five-year-old Stuart Lockwood from the UK. Stuart was held in Iraq for four months as part of Saddam Hussein's "human shield."*

Terrorism

Some hostage-takers don't wish to negotiate. They seize hostages to create a climate of fear and terror among a local population in order to subdue them, or to frighten away foreigners. Hostages in these situations are at great risk because their captors have very little to lose. The hostage may even be killed to show that the threat is real. No motive was ever found for the abduction and murder of Irish aid worker Margaret Hassan in Iraq in 2004, but many suspected that an Islamist terrorist organization opposed to the Allied invasion of Iraq was responsible.

BUSTED!

Colombian politician Ingrid Betancourt was captured by the Colombian Revolutionary People's Party (FARC) in 2002 and held captive in the jungle for over six years. She and several U.S. hostages were eventually released when members of the Colombian military intelligence managed to infiltrate local FARC squads. The captors were duped into allowing the hostages to board an unmarked helicopter manned by soldiers disguised as FARC fighters.

FACT FILE

The first concern for police officers faced with a hostage crisis is always the safety of the hostage. In order to decide on an appropriate response, they must therefore establish the hostage-taker's motives, which may include the following:

- self-protection—the hostage provides a human shield

- winning political or military concessions

- gaining publicity for their cause

- creating a climate of fear

- as punishment or revenge

▶ *Freed hostage Ingrid Betancourt (see Busted box) is reunited with her son and daughter in Bogota, Colombia, in July 2008.*

CASE STUDY: LEBANON

For most of the 1980s, Lebanon, a small country in the Middle East, was engulfed by civil war. It was a very dangerous place, and militant groups backed by Iran and Syria seized dozens of foreign hostages in a prolonged campaign to gain concessions from western countries.

Motives

The civil war in Lebanon was fought between different Lebanese factions and Palestinians, with intervention from Israel, the U.S., Iran, and Syria. Some extreme Islamist groups backed by Iran began to take hostages as insurance against retaliation by the West for various atrocities committed in the capital, Beirut. They also wanted various terrorists held in Kuwait and elsewhere to be released, and to force the U.S. to do something about the Israeli invasion of southern Lebanon.

▼ *Beirut, the war-torn capital of Lebanon, in 1982. The bombed-out apartment blocks and cellars provided plenty of places to conceal kidnap victims.*

Tactics

One of the most dramatic hostage-takings involved the hijacking of a U.S. plane from Cairo to London in June 1985 (see pages 30–31 for more information on hijacking). Dozens of passengers were captured and held in Beirut for two weeks before they were released. However, most kidnappings involved just one or two victims, often journalists, teachers, or diplomats working in Beirut. Their kidnappers moved them from secret location to secret location, often forcing them to endure appalling conditions, beatings, and mock executions. Almost all victims were chosen not because of anything they had done, but simply because of the country they came from.

Secret Negotiations

The sprawling city of Beirut was under the control of different factions. Some hostages were smuggled out of the city and many were held for several years. No foreign government wanted to admit to making deals with the hostage-takers, but political pressure was mounting for something to be done and the release of a number of Lebanese militants during this time suggests that countries such as Israel and France were involved in secret negotiations. President Ronald Reagan even negotiated a secret and illegal arms deal with Iran in an attempt to stop the kidnapping of U.S. citizens in Lebanon.

The End

By the early 1990s, the Lebanese civil war had ended, many Islamist militants had been freed from prison, and Iran, one of the states that had fueled the conflict, now wanted to encourage Western investment to repair its struggling economy. The remaining hostages had outlived their usefulness and the last hostage was released in December 1991.

FACT FILE

- The Lebanon hostage crisis lasted from 1982–1991.

- During this time, 96 hostages from 21 different countries were captured, including 25 Americans.

- At least eight foreign hostages died while being held.

- Terry Waite, a British envoy sent to negotiate hostage release, was held for five years—four of which were spent in solitary confinement. Terry Anderson, a U.S. journalist, was held for nearly seven years— the longest of any of the hostages.

- Thousands of Lebanese hostages were also captured during the civil war. Many have disappeared without a trace.

► U.S. hostage Terry Anderson (center) raises his hand on his return to New York after his release. He was held in Beirut for nearly seven years.

HIJACKING

Hijacking can be seen as a form of piracy. It is the illegal seizure of a plane, ship, or truck. Criminals usually hijack ships and trucks for profit, but most plane hijackers have different motives. They may want safe passage to a particular destination. They may want to use the passengers and crew as bargaining tools to obtain concessions. Sometimes they simply want publicity for their cause. However, the last decade has seen a disturbing rise in vehicles hijacked for use as an attack weapon.

Terrorists' Demands

The hijacking of aircraft was extremely rare until the late 1960s, when commercial flights became much more frequent and militant groups such as the Palestinian Liberation Organization first began to use it as a terror tactic to gain concessions and publicity. One of the most notorious hijacks from this period occurred in 1976 when Palestinian militants hijacked a plane en route from Israel to France. The hijackers forced the plane, which was carrying many Jewish passengers, to land in Entebbe, Uganda. Non-Jewish passengers were freed, but the

▼ An injured survivor of the Entebbe hijacking returns to Tel Aviv, Israel, in July 1976.

hijackers said the remaining passengers would be killed if their demands for the release of Palestinian prisoners held in Israel were not met. One week later, a rescue mission by Israeli defense forces resulted in the release of the remaining passengers. Four hostages and all of the hijackers were killed during the rescue.

Preventative Measures

Before the terrorist attacks on the United States in September 2001 (see pages 32–33), airport security relied on metal detectors and physical searches to prevent potential hijackers taking guns, knives, or other weapons onto a plane. If a hijacker did attempt to take control of a plane mid-flight, the crew

ON TARGET

The United States and Cuba were uneasy neighbors in the 1960s, and there were a number of plane hijackings between the two countries. These incidents decreased at the end of the 1970s with the introduction of these measures:

- an amendment to Cuban law in 1970 that made hijacking a crime

- the introduction of metal detectors in U.S. airports

- an agreement between the United States and Cuba to return or prosecute all hijackers

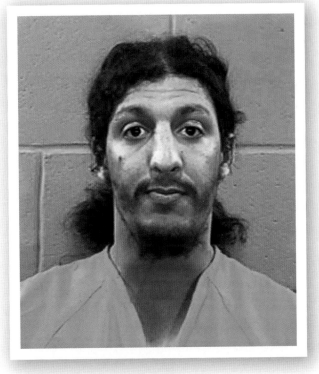

▲ The "shoe bomber" Richard Reid after his arrest in December 2001.

was instructed to fly the plane as directed and leave any counter-measures to the security forces on the ground once the plane had landed. After the 9/11 attacks, when four planes were hijacked and used as attack weapons, all of this changed. Crews are now given specific training to overcome hijackers on board (see page 38).

Suicide Bombers

A suicide bomber is someone who uses explosives to blow up themselves and others, either as a means of attacking their enemies or to gain publicity for their cause. Many of the recent measures designed to deter hijackers are also intended to stop suicide bombers such as Richard Reid, the British "shoe bomber," who tried to blow up a plane in December 2001 by igniting explosives hidden in his shoe. As a result, all plane passengers must now remove their shoes for inspection before boarding a flight.

BUSTED!

In August 2006, a terrorist plot to blow up a number of transatlantic planes was uncovered after a year-long surveillance operation by British security services. Because the bombs were made from liquid explosives, new security measures included a ban on passengers carrying liquids onto planes. The bombers' ring-leader, Abdulla Ahmed Ali, was sentenced to 40 years in prison.

CASE STUDY: 9/11

International attitudes to security changed dramatically on September 11, 2001, when al-Qaeda terrorists hijacked four planes and used them as weapons to attack targets in the United States. Nearly 3,000 people died as a result of the attacks. The repercussions were far-reaching. The U.S. allies declared a "war on terror" and security strategies all over the world were adjusted accordingly.

Preparations

The 19 hijackers, all from Saudi Arabia, the United Arab Emirates, Lebanon, and Egypt, prepared extensively for the attacks. They received lessons in English and western culture at al-Qaeda training camps in Afghanistan, and those chosen to be pilots trained at schools in California. The others were recruited as "muscle" to help subdue the crew and passengers. They all bought legitimate first class tickets for scheduled flights, and did not attempt to conceal their identities from the airlines.

▼ Hijacked United Airlines Flight 175 from Boston crashes into the south tower of the World Trade Center on September 11, 2001, in New York City.

ON TARGET

The chances of a successful hijack on U.S. flights have now been reduced, according to the Transportation Security Administration (TSA), because of three main developments:

- the use of bullet-proof cockpit doors to prevent forced entry

- armed pilots and armed marshals on some flights

- improved passenger awareness of suspicious behavior

Each country sets their own security requirements. Airport security in Israel is generally regarded as the most rigorous in the world, but other countries don't necessarily apply the same vigilance.

◀ Airport police officers armed with rifles stand guard as international travelers wait in line at Los Angeles International Airport.

Coordinated Attacks

Once the targeted planes were airborne on the morning of September 11, a number of passengers and crew managed to send messages or make cell phone calls and revealed that the attackers used knives and fake bombs to take control of the planes. Two of the planes crashed shortly afterwards into the World Trade Center in New York. A third plane crashed into the Pentagon near Washington, DC. The hijackers of the fourth plane may have intended to crash it into the White House, but passengers and crew managed to fight back, and the plane came down in rural Pennsylvania instead. Everyone on board all four planes was killed.

Changes to Security

The Transportation Security Administration (TSA) was established after 9/11. They review and implement a wide range of new security measures to stop potential hijackers boarding planes. These include prescreening passenger details to highlight suspicious activity, more physical checks and electronic detectors before boarding, greater police presence at airports, and better cooperation between airlines and security officials.

BUSTED!

In 2006, a U.S. court sentenced Zacarias Moussaoui to life imprisonment for his part in plotting an attack in a fifth plane on 9/11. He did not take part in the attacks themselves because he had already been arrested after acting suspiciously at flight school. However, the court decided that he could have saved many lives if he had revealed details of the plot to the police.

NEGOTIATION

Hijacking, piracy, kidnapping, and hostage-taking are serious crimes. But when innocent civilians are held and threatened, law enforcement agencies have to proceed with great caution. Their primary goal is usually the safe release of any hostages and the non-violent surrender of the criminals.

Private Negotiation

Of course, the easiest way to achieve the victims' safe release may be to agree to the hostage-takers' demands. Thousands of kidnappings do end in this way each year, when families simply pay the ransom that is demanded without involving the police. But all of the evidence from countries with high kidnapping rates suggests that giving in to such demands merely encourages further kidnappings.

Involving the Police

Many law enforcement agencies have trained negotiators, who are available 24 hours a day, to respond to hostage crises or kidnapping incidents. A negotiator's job is to obtain the safe release of any hostages without making major concessions. This can involve a number of tactics, including the following:

- establishing and maintaining calm, open communication with the hostage-takers

- gaining information about the hostage-takers and their environment

- exploring alternative outcomes and options to those demanded by the hostage-takers

- lowering the expectations of the hostage-takers

This approach is incorporated in the motto of the FBI Negotiation Unit which is "resolution through dialogue."

▼ Police negotiators at work in Kansas

Government Responses

Some governments are prepared to negotiate with hostage-takers in order to secure the release of their own nationals. This may mean giving in to their demands. For example, President Arroyo of the Philippines secured the release of a Filipino truck driver kidnapped in Iraq by agreeing to move up the scheduled departure of Filipino troops in 2004.

The United Kingdom, on the other hand, has a long-standing policy of making no concessions to kidnappers or hostage-takers. When Somali pirates kidnapped a British couple, Paul and Rachel Chandler, from their yacht in the Indian Ocean in 2009, the British government confirmed their policy remained unchanged. The Chandlers were released in November 2010 after a privately-funded ransom was paid to the kidnappers.

▼ *Paul and Rachel Chandler before their kidnapping in October 2009.*

▲ *Freed Filipino truck driver Angelo de la Cruz is reunited with his family in July 2004.*

ON TARGET

United Nations General-Secretary Ban Ki-Moon has expressed his desire to establish common rules between nations on making deals with hostage-takers. This followed complaints from the United States that in 2007, Italy released five captured Taliban fighters in exchange for a kidnapped Italian journalist. However, other countries have argued that the right of individual nations to protect the lives of their citizens as they see fit must be protected.

ARMED RESPONSE

Sometimes negotiations with hostage-takers break down. And sometimes negotiation isn't even a possibility if the hostage-taker is a suicide bomber whose ideology leaves no room for compromise. When this happens, the only option for law enforcement agencies is armed response.

Working with Negotiators

In many hostage crises, negotiators and armed response teams work alongside each other. The negotiators focus on gaining more time, obtaining intelligence about any weapons, the exact whereabouts of the hostages and whether there is any possibility of voluntary surrender. The response team can then assess the likelihood of a successful attack and rescue attempt.

▼ *This picture shows several of the Chechen militants who took part in the 2002 Moscow theater siege wearing explosives strapped to their bodies. Their leader, Movsar Barayev, (unmasked) talks to TV journalists from inside the theater building.*

The Moscow Theater Siege

The success of any armed response to something as unpredictable as a hostage crisis is never guaranteed. In October 2002, 40 to 50 armed militants from Chechnya (a region to the south of Russia) invaded a theater in the Russian capital, Moscow. The heavily-armed militants held around 850 people hostage for two and a half days, threatening to kill the hostages if Russia did not withdraw its troops from Chechnya. A tense period of negotiation ensued, with a number of famous politicians and journalists intervening in discussions and some hostages speaking to radio stations on their cell phones.

Strong Response

Meanwhile, Russian Special Forces were preparing for an armed response. On the morning of October 26, they began their attack by pumping poisonous gas into the theater. Afterwards, the Russian president Putin declared the action to be successful in terms of freeing the hostages, but over 100 innocent people were killed by the gas, and none of the militants left the building alive.

A Difficult Debate

How should a government respond when hijackers take control of a plane and threaten to crash it into a crowded building or city? A new law passed in Germany in 2005 allowed "direct action by armed force" against a hijacked aircraft. However, this law was later overturned, because the shooting down of a plane full of innocent people was deemed to be state-sponsored murder, even if such action was intended to save many more innocent lives.

BUSTED!

In December 1994, four Islamic militants hijacked an Air France plane in Algiers, North Africa and forced it to fly to Marseilles in France. Once on the ground in Marseilles, French special operations police (GIGN) disguised as airport workers planted listening devices while delivering supplies. They learned that the hijackers hoped to fly the plane to Paris and possibly crash it into the Eiffel Tower. Negotiators then pretended to arrange a press conference at the front of the plane and asked the hijackers to move the hostages to the rear. The GIGN stormed the plane, killing all four hijackers. Over a dozen hostages were injured during the rescue, but overall, it was considered a success.

▼ A hijacked Air France plane is stormed by police at Marseilles airport in December 1994.

TRAINING AND SUPPORT

Many countries maintain specialized armed response teams to deal with hostage situations. However, achieving a successful outcome can depend on the behavior of the hostages, as well as the professionalism of the negotiators and armed response teams.

Precautions at Sea

With the recent dramatic rise in piracy in the Gulf of Aden, ship owners, insurance companies, and law enforcement agencies have all urged crews to take a few basic steps to protect themselves in the event of an attack. These steps include pulling up all ladders while at sea, changing course, speeding up, and firing flares to avoid capture, and maintaining a safe room on board with food, water, and communications equipment. Increasing numbers of ships are also now sailing with additional trained security personnel on board.

▲ The FBI Hostage Rescue Team trains year-round to prepare for a crisis in any location.

Training Air Crew

After the plane hijackings of September 11, 2001, many airlines, including all U.S. airlines, reassessed the training they gave to inflight crew members in the event of an attempted hijack or suicide bombing. The TSA now provides self-defense training for all crew and encourages direct action to avert disaster, rather than passive compliance with a hijacker's demands.

ON TARGET

In 2006, the United Nations Office on Drugs and Crime (UNODC) launched a manual to help countries deal with the problem of kidnapping and hostage-taking. The manual is intended to give police and policy-makers guidance on how to respond to kidnappings, develop preventative measures, and draw up effective legislation to deal with kidnappers. UNODC executive director Antonio Maria Costa has said that "the purpose of this manual is to save lives."

Civilians at Risk

Statistically, kidnapping victims are most likely to be harmed in the first hour of their ordeal. Civilians, such as journalists, aid workers, diplomats, and engineers traveling to work in "high risk" regions of the world, such as some countries in Asia, Africa, and the Middle East, are often offered some form of self-defense or risk assessment training by their employers to help them avoid being kidnapped. They are also taught techniques to help them to cope more successfully if they are kidnapped.

BUSTED!

In May 2010, the oil-tanker *Moscow University* was attacked by armed Somali pirates in the Gulf of Aden. The 23-member crew immediately locked themselves into the engine room, which meant the pirates could not control the movement of the ship. A Russian warship in the area responded to the crew's distress calls by sending a helicopter to investigate. When the helicopter had established that the crew was safely out of the way, it fired on the pirates, who surrendered.

▼ *These people aren't police officers—they are pilots who have volunteered for specialist weapons training with the TSA in Brunswick, Georgia.*

SURVIVING A KIDNAPPING

The majority of kidnapping victims and hostages are released eventually. This is either because their captors' demands are met, they escape, or they are rescued by the police or military response units. Sometimes there is a blaze of publicity. Sometimes the public isn't even aware that a kidnapping had taken place. But the involvement of outside agencies does not end when the victim walks free.

Debriefing

When a kidnapping victim or hostage is released, they are usually interviewed by police or government embassy staff to try to establish what happened, who their captors were, and where they were held. This helps police trace the kidnappers and provides vital information about how such an incident might be avoided in the future. When British hostage Peter Moore was freed in 2009 after nearly three years in captivity in Iraq, he was immediately taken for debriefing by the UK's Metropolitan Police where he gave detectives and psychiatrists his account of what happened to him and the four bodyguards who were murdered during the ordeal.

Counseling

Kidnapping victims and hostages are often subjected to long periods of isolation, physical threats, and psychological trauma during their captivity. The joy and relief that comes with their release can mask deep scars. Many victims need special counseling to help them come to terms with their experiences. Some government agencies and charities are beginning to offer this kind of support. A third of the world's commercial sailors come from the Philippines, and its Overseas Workers Welfare Administration now offers counseling to any sailors who are victims of pirate attacks.

◄ Freed British hostage Peter Moore (left) arrives at a Royal Air Force base in the United Kingdom, two days after his release in December 2009.

▲ Austrian kidnapping victim Natascha Kampusch talks to journalists in 2010, two years after she successfully escaped from the abductor who had held her in a cellar for eight years.

Stockholm Syndrome

Psychologists have identified a type of behavior where some hostage victims become emotionally attached to their captors, despite the trauma and suffering inflicted on them. This type of behavior seems completely irrational, yet may occur because the victim is isolated and dependent and starts to feel grateful for the fact that they have not been killed and are "valued" by their captors. Austrian Natascha Kampusch and American Jaycee Dugard (see On Target box) were both kidnapped as children, and both women have shown some positive feelings towards their captors. According to the FBI's data, 27 percent of all hostages show some evidence for what is commonly called Stockholm Syndrome.

ON TARGET

Eleven-year-old Jaycee Dugard was abducted and held for 18 years by Phillip and Nancy Garrido (see page 24). However, Phillip Garrido was under supervision by parole officers for about ten years of that time, and they failed to spot irregularities in his behavior and responses. In 2010, the State of California accepted responsibility and the Dugard family was awarded $20 million in damages, in part to pay for long-term therapy to help them recover from their ordeal.

GLOSSARY

abduction another word for kidnapping, often used to describe the kidnapping of a child

al-Qaeda an Islamist terrorist movement originating in Afghanistan and the Middle East

Barbary An area on the North African coast that was famous for its pirates.

circumstantial evidence proof presented at a trial that aims to persuade a jury of the defendant's guilt; unlike direct evidence, such as a fingerprint, circumstantial evidence cannot directly prove a defendant's guilt.

civilian any non-military person

civil war war between people living in the same country

commercial used for trade or business

concessions advantages gained through negotiation

corruption criminal activity by officials who exploit their position; taking bribes

developed countries countries where the majority of the population is comparatively wealthy and the economy is founded more on industry than on agriculture

developing countries countries where the majority of the population is comparatively poor and the economy is still founded more on agriculture than on industry

diplomats officials appointed by the government to represent their country's interests abroad

GPS (Global Positioning System) a navigational system that uses satellites to locate positions around the world

grappling hook a tool with lots of hooks that is used to grab something; it is often thrown on the end of a rope.

guerrilla rebel fighter

hijacking the illegal seizure of a plane, ship, or truck

hostage a kidnapping victim who is held against his or her will

ideology a set of ideas that form the basis of a political, economic, or religious system

infiltrate gain access secretly

jurisdiction area of legal control

lucrative financially rewarding

militant prepared to fight

negotiator someone who is in direct communication with both sides in a conflict or a hostage crisis

overhead operating costs; in a kidnapping, these would include the cost of keeping the victim hidden and making sure they have sufficient food

press-gang a historic practice of forcing people to work on board ships

privateers pirates who are permitted to operate by their government in exchange for a share of the profits

ransom money demanded by kidnappers in exchange for their victims' release

skiff fishing boat

solitary confinement imprisonment without access to other prisoners

surveillance watching and listening, usually in secret

transatlantic slave trade the shipment of people from Africa to the Americas for the purposes of slavery; this trade was made illegal in the 19th century.

waterways oceans, channels, lakes, and rivers

FURTHER INFORMATION

Books

Burns, Jan. *Kidnapping (Crime Scene Investigations),* Lucent Books, 2008.

Pipe, Jim. *Pirates (True Stories and Legends),* Stargazer Books, 2010.

Porterfield, Jason. *Modern-Day Piracy (In the News),* Rosen Pub. Group, 2010.

Rooney, Anne. *Kidnaps (Solve It with Science),* Smart Apple Media, 2010.

Web Sites

www.amberalert.gov
A web site that links the police and the media to get the message out quickly when a child goes missing.

http://independent.co.uk/news/world/africa/history-of-piracy-on-the-high-seas_1023701.html
Facts and figures on pirates both past and present.

http://english.aljazeera.net/news/africa/2008/11/2008111971844162942.html
Background information on piracy in the Gulf of Aden.

www.cusnc.navy.mil/cmf/151/index.html
Information, photos and stories about Combined Task Force 151.

www.un.org/terrorism
News and reports on what the UN is doing to combat terrorism.

http://news.bbc.co.uk/1/hi/world/europe/2363601.stm
A report on the Moscow theater siege in 2002.

http://news.bbc.co.uk/1/hi/uk/8572441.stm
The story of Sahil Saeed's kidnap and rescue.

www.bbc.co.uk/news/uk-10338484
The timeline of Paul and Rachel Chandler's kidnap and release.

INDEX

SERIES CONTENTS

Cybercrime Inside Picture • Hacking • Case Study: Gary McKinnon • Phishing • Cyberbullying • Cyberstalking • Virus Attacks • Malware • Social Networking Sites • Fraudulent Web Sites • Denial-of-Service Attacks • Identity Theft • Case Study: Pirate Bay • Cyberterrorism • Cyber Wars • Case Study: Cyber Wars in Eastern Europe • Cybersecurity

Drug Crime Drug Crime: A Worldwide Problem • Which Drugs Are Illegal? • Who Are the Criminals? • The Flow of Drugs • The Cost of Drugs • Tackling the Traffickers • Smuggling and Mules • Case Study: Below the Waves! • Stop and Search • Global Drug Watch • Surveillance • Case Study: Operation Junglefowl • Going Undercover • The Bust • Case Study: Operation Habitat • Rehabilitation • The Future

Forensics Inside Picture • Fingerprinting • Securing the Crime Scene • The Autopsy • Natural Clues: Insects • Soils and Seeds • Using Blood • DNA Evidence • Bones and Skulls • Case Study: The Body Farm • Clothes and Shoes • Paper Trail • Guns and Bullets • Drugs and Poisons • Crash Investigations • Fire Investigations • Case Study: Lockerbie Bombing

Gun Crime Gun Crime—Out of Control? • What Is Gun Crime? • What Guns Are Used? • Who Commits Gun Crimes? • Case Study: Killing Sprees • How Much Gun Crime Is There? • Getting Hold of Guns • Controls and Penalties • Arming the Police • War on the Streets • Solving Gun Crime • Firearms in the Crime Lab • Case Study: The Washington Sniper • Tackling Gun Crime • Case Study: Operation Trident • Gun Crime in the Media • An Ongoing Debate

Juvenile Crime Inside Picture • Changing Times • Cracking Down on Kids • Everybody Does It! • The Problem with Sex • The Alcohol Demon • Drugs and Young People • Gangs • Case Study: Youth Gangs in South Africa • Armed and Dangerous • Children Who Kill • Case Study: The Story of Mary Bell • School and College Massacres • On Trial • Locked Up • Alternatives to Prison • Prevention Is Better Than Cure

Kidnapping and Piracy Inside Picture • In the Past • Piracy at Sea • Somalia • Case Study: MV Sirius Star • Policing the Pirates • Prosecution and Detention • Kidnapping for Ransom • Abducting Children • Taken Hostage • Case Study: Lebanon • Hijacking • Case Study: 9/11 • Negotiation • Armed Response • Training and Support • Surviving a Kidnapping

People Trafficking Inside Picture • How Did We Get Here? • The Traffickers • The Victims • Forced Labor • The Sex Industry • Trafficking Children • Source Countries • In Transit • Border Controls • Case Study: The European Union • Caught in the Act • Loopholes in the Law • Police and Welfare • Working with NGOs • Raising Awareness • Taking a Stand

Policing and Justice What Is Criminal Justice? • Rough Justice • Enforcing the Law • Dealing with Serious Crimes • Officers of the Law • Case Study: Racism by the Police • Guarding the Guardians • Case Study: Reforming the Police • The Criminal Justice System • Arrest and Detention • Seeking Justice: The Courts • Punishment • Alternatives to Prison • Juvenile Justice • Case Study: Dealing with Terrorism • Victims' Rights • The Future